WOLFGANG AMADEUS
MOZART

Richard Tames

Franklin Watts

London ● New York ● Sydney ● Toronto

Contents

Franklin Watts 1991

First published in Great Britain
in 1991 by
Franklin Watts
96 Leonard Street
London EC2A 4RH

First published in the USA by
Franklin Watts Inc.
387 Park Avenue South
New York, N.Y. 10016

First published in Australia by
Franklin Watts
14 Mars Road
Lane Cove
NSW 2066

UK ISBN: 0 7496 0266 X

Phototypeset by: JB Type, Hove, East Sussex
Printed in: Belgium
Series Editor: Hazel Poole
Designed by: Nick Cannan

A CIP catalogue record for this book is available from
the British Library.

A Musical Family

If ever a creative artist deserved the title of "genius" it is Mozart. When it came to music he was simply outstanding at everything he attempted. He could play both stringed and keyboard instruments to perfection. He could improvise by the hour and memorize a whole composition from a single hearing, and his own compositions covered every musical form from masses to operas, from symphonies to string quartets. He amazed the world with his dazzling skills as a performer when only a child. Since his tragic early death, the music he composed has enriched the lives of millions. Almost every scrap of anything he wrote has been recorded, in most cases many times over. Music-lovers for two centuries, it seems, could never have too much of Mozart. But in his own day it was not always so. Triumph and tragedy marched hand in hand throughout his brief but brilliant career. Mozart was born into a family of musicians. His father, Leopold, not only played and taught the **clavier**, organ and violin but, in the year of Wolfgang's birth, published a textbook about learning the violin. This became a standard work on the subject and made the family name of Mozart well-known among musicians far beyond Salzburg, where Leopold was official composer at the court of the Prince-Archbishop.

Most of Leopold Mozart's children died in infancy. Only two survived.

Leopold Mozart — a loving and proud father, but strict, snobbish and a hard task-master.

The oldest, Anna Maria Wallurga was born in 1751. Her nickname was "Nannerl". The seventh and last child, a boy, was born on 27 January 1756 and christened Johann Chrysostom Wolfgang Theophilus. Later this was shortened to Wolfgang Amadeus. Amadeus is the Latin version of the Greek name Theophilus and the German name Gottlieb. They all mean "lover of God." The boy was given the nickname of "Wolfgangerl", which was then shortened to "Woferl".

Nannerl began to learn the

This picture of the Mozart family playing together actually dates from 1777 — when Mozart was 21!

clavier when she was five and soon proved to be so good that Leopold had high hopes for her. When Wolfgang was four he began to take an interest in his sister's lessons. He had been playing with musical instruments for more than a year and Leopold now realized that the little boy could start to learn properly. He was soon amazed by his son's progress, as Wolfgang quickly mastered the principles of keyboard and stringed instruments and showed that he had a perfect sense of pitch. He also began to make up compositions of his own, even before he knew how to write them down for himself. His father wrote out for him the first piece he ever composed, a minuet.

When Wolfgang was nearly six and his sister eleven, their father decided that it was time to show them off to the world. In January 1762, the whole family set off for Munich, where the Elector of Bavaria's court was famed for its music. Their arrival was timed for the height of the carnival season, when there were concerts and parties every night. Their concert was a great success. Wolfgang's trick of playing the clavier while the keys were covered with a piece of cloth became the talk of the town. The family was invited to all the great houses and palaces to perform. But, for Wolfgang, this was far less exciting than being taken to the opera for the first time. He was entranced.

The Mozarts' success in Munich was far greater than Leopold had dared to hope for. They had returned with applause ringing in their ears — and money in their pockets. Next he set his sights on Vienna, the most important city in all of central Europe, where the Emperor himself held court. When it actually came to giving a concert in the Emperor's presence, it was the audience which was overawed and not the young Mozart:

" ... the audience could scarcely believe their eyes and ears when the children played. In particular, the Emperor, Francis I, was delighted with the little wizard, as he jokingly called him". The tiny child even ordered the Emperor to move off his piano bench when he sat next to him so that someone else could turn the pages of his music for him.

When the Emperor challenged Wolfgang to play a piece with one finger "resolutely he tried it at once and to everyone's astonishment played several pieces very neatly in this manner". He also proposed marriage to the little Princess

A family portrait of 1780/81 includes the Mozarts' mother. Note that Mozart and his sister are playing a cross-handed duet.

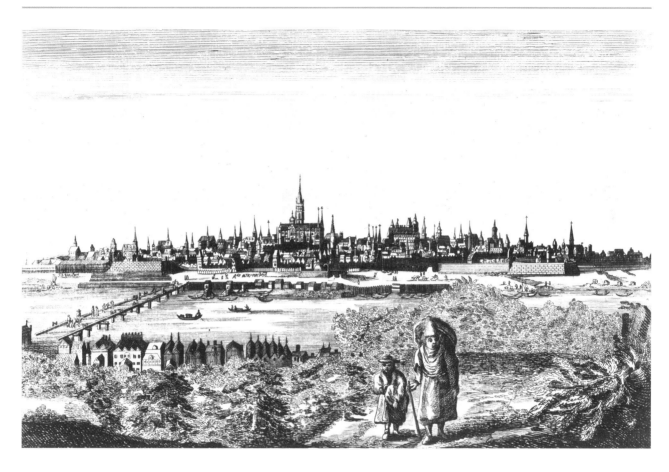

Marie Antoinette, the future tragic queen of France and when the time came to say goodbye, "the little wizard" went right up to the Empress, "jumped on her lap, threw his arms round her neck and kissed her good and thoroughly". The following week was filled with demands for concerts and the strain soon showed on the little boy, who went down with a fever and a rash and had to stay in bed for two weeks. This interval was enough to make the nobility lose interest in the one-week wonder. So Leopold decided to head back to Salzburg. He had got what he had come for — the Emperor's applause and an invitation to repeat the triumph in France.

Vienna around 1750, the capital of a great empire of many peoples but still close to the countryside.
(Below) **The Vienna Opera House — still the pride of a city renowned for its love of music.**

In June 1763, the Mozarts set out on a tour which was to last three and a half years. Leopold himself wrote the advertisement for their extraordinary concerts:

"The little girl who is in her twelfth year, will play the most difficult compositions of the greatest masters; the boy who is not yet 7 will perform ... on the harpsichord: he will also play a **concerto** for the violin ... he will instantly name all notes played at a distance, whether singly or in chords, on the clavier, or any other instrument, glass bell or clock. He will finally, both on the harpsichord and the organ, improvise as long as may be desired and in any key ... "

After performing in half a dozen major German cities, the family at last reached Paris in November. Less than two weeks after their arrival, Melchior Grimm (1723-1807), a famous writer, published a glowing account of Wolfgang's skills.

On New Year's Day 1764, the Mozarts were summoned to dine with King Louis XV at the Palace of Versailles. Leopold recorded with obvious delight:

"My Wolfgang was graciously privileged to stand beside the Queen the whole time, to talk constantly to her, entertain her and kiss her hands repeatedly, beside partaking of the dishes which she handed him from the table."

Wolfgang then played to great applause. As usual, once Royal approval had been given, the family

Mozart aged seven — poised, self-confident and dressed as a courtier — right down to the sword.

was showered with invitations from the nobility and gave two public concerts which proved to be a great financial success.

After Paris came London, where they stayed for over a year and made more money than they had ever had before. King George III was a great music-lover and Queen Charlotte had appointed Johann Christian Bach, son of the great

Central Europe, showing today's national borders. Mozart's music still appeals across all frontiers.

Johann Sebastian Bach, as her music master. The city had a positive passion for Italian operas and had attracted many of the most famous Italian singers of the day. The Mozarts went to hear as many as they could and Wolfgang began to dream of the day when he, too, would write an opera in the Italian style. In the meantime, he composed six sonatas for violin and harpsichord and dedicated them to Queen Charlotte, who gave him the handsome sum of 50 guineas.

From London the Mozarts went to The Hague, capital of the Netherlands. Here Nannerl fell very ill, probably from typhoid. Feverish and delirious, she seemed to be just wasting away. Her family expected her to die, but to their joy, she slowly recovered. Then Wolfgang fell ill in the same way. Leopold noted with alarm that the disease "in 4 weeks has made him so wretched that he is not only absolutely unrecognizable but has nothing left but his tender skin on his little bones". He hovered near death until, with careful nursing, he began to make a slow recovery. In due course, however, these severe bouts of childhood illness were to take their toll.

After their recovery, Wolfgang and Nannerl performed briefly but successfully in The Hague before moving on to Paris once more. In Paris their old friend Melchior Grimm predicted of Wolfgang that "before he is twelve years old he will already have an opera

Salzburg in Mozart's day. Today it hosts an annual Mozart festival.

performed in some Italian theatre". He also noted that, besides his almost miraculous skills as a player and immense promise as a composer, the young Mozart took a lively interest in people and places, spoke excellent French, English and Italian as well as his native German, and had a proper boyish sense of fun. He also adored his parents and took more pleasure in pleasing them than in all the praise showered upon him by admirers.

After Paris, the Mozarts returned to Salzburg via Switzerland, giving concerts along the way. Their tour had made Wolfgang famous throughout Europe and he was still only 10 years old.

In Salzburg, young Mozart devoted himself to schoolwork and composition until his father decided that they should go to Vienna, where the Princess Marie Josepha was to be married. Music would be needed for the festivities. It would be another chance for the child-wonder to shine. But an outbreak of smallpox killed the young princess and cleared the city of its frightened inhabitants, although the Mozarts were not quick enough in leaving and both Wolfgang and Nannerl were once again severely ill for some time with the deadly disease.

In January 1768, when Wolfgang was just 12, the Mozarts returned to Vienna where the new Emperor, Joseph II, suggested that Wolfgang should write an Italian opera. The result was *La Finta Semplice* (*The Pretended Simpleton*). But it was not to be performed. Rival composers, outraged at the very idea of a 12 year old writing an opera, managed to persuade the orchestra and singers that no child could possibly write music worth performing.

Bitterly disappointed, young Wolfgang packed up the 558 pages of manuscript he had written and returned to Salzburg, where the kindly Archbishop arranged a performance on 1 May 1769. It was a great success.

Modern Salzburg retains much of its ancient elegance.

Johann Christian Bach 1735-83

Johann Christian Bach was the youngest son of the great Johann Sebastian Bach and therefore a member of the most talented musical family Europe has ever seen. After playing church music and writing operas in Italy, he was invited to London. The wife of the new king, George III, was a fellow German and she appointed Bach as her music master. His duties included teaching her to play the harpsichord, accompanying the king when he played the flute and teaching music to the ever-growing family of Royal children.

Bach, who had no children of his own, was a great favourite in London and used his influence generously on Mozart's behalf. The two of them got on very well together. Mozart is supposed to have said to his sister "I think Johann Christian Bach is by far the nicest man I have ever met. I'm composing a symphony in the style he uses". This was his first symphony.

Bach and Mozart also delighted Londoners with a "double-act" in which, with the boy sitting on the man's knees, they would improvise together, sitting at the same clavier, for two hours at a time.

Like Mozart, Bach was to find that his great popularity simply began to fade one day and, like Mozart, he continued to live beyond his means and died in great debt.

Like his country-man, Handel, Johann Christian Bach found fame and fortune in his adopted country. Unlike Handel, he lost the fortune.

The Making of a Maestro

Mozart and his father left for Italy, the home of opera and heart of European music, in December 1769. They arrived in Verona in time for the carnival season. Mozart's first public concert was an instant sensation. In Milan it was the same story, with the added bonus of a commission to write a new opera for the following year's carnival celebrations.

In Bologna the Mozarts visited Padre Martini, the most respected music expert in Europe. Every test of knowledge or performance the maestro could devise, young Mozart handled with ease, to the old man's great delight. In Rome, Wolfgang enjoyed seeing the sights but still found time to compose two arias and three symphonies. After a month in Naples it was back to Rome again to meet the Pope, who gave the young genius the Order of the Golden Spur. In theory Wolfgang was now "Signor Cavaliere", a knight, but he never used the title. The only other musician ever to have received this honour was the Emperor's official composer, Gluck.

Returning to Bologna, Mozart sat an examination for the Accademia Filarmonica, an exclusive brotherhood of the most distinguished musicians. Normally applicants had to be over 21 to take the examination. In Mozart's case the rule was ignored. The task set for him normally took over 3 hours. He

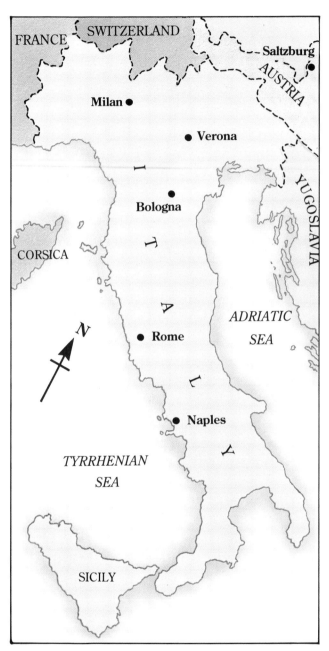

Italy (shown here with its modern frontiers) gave Europe the technical language of music.

finished it in 30 minutes. Needless to say, his test composition won him immediate election as an honorary member of the academy.

Mozart, wearing the Papal Order of the Golden Spur.

Back in Milan, Mozart set to work to complete his opera — *Mithridatus, King of Pontus* — based on a tragedy by the French writer, Racine. The first performance was given the day after Christmas, with the composer himself conducting, as well as playing the clavier. It was another triumph and was followed by 20 more performances. As a result of this great success, Mozart was commissioned to write yet another opera and music for the wedding of Milan's Archduke Ferdinand, scheduled for October 1771.

After spending the spring and summer in Salzburg, composing busily, Mozart returned to Italy with his father in the autumn. His music for the Royal wedding, an operatic ballet *Ascanio in Alba*, was so hugely applauded that he received not only his fee but also a bonus, a gold watch studded with diamonds. But the one thing that Leopold wanted for his son was still out of reach — a permanent post as the Archduke's court musician. So they returned to Salzburg in time for Christmas.

In the spring of 1772, the Mozarts' kind and generous patron, the Archbishop of Salzburg, suddenly died. He had allowed both father and son a great deal of freedom to make their fortune and develop their talents. His successor, Archbishop Hieronymous Joseph von Paula, Count von Colloredo, was to prove a far less easy-going master. Although he did allow them to return to Milan to present Mozart's second major opera, *Lucio Silla*. Two weeks later Leopold wrote "Thank God, the opera is an extraordinary success and every day the theatre is surprisingly full".

Mozart was now 17. Would his talents progress and develop into maturity? Or would time expose him as a child wonder and nothing more ? The next phase of his life was to temper his character as well as his talent.

Archbishop Colloredo began to

Haydn, composer of over 100 symphonies, painted during one of his two visits to England.

make it very clear that he found the Mozart's to be a family with far too high an opinion of themselves. He took the traditional, aristocratic view that musicians, however talented, were only servants. Nevertheless, he continued to allow them to travel. Wolfgang re-visited Vienna where, for the first time, he heard the music of Joseph Haydn, which made a deep impression on him. In January 1775, Mozart presented a new opera, *La Finta Giardiniera* (*The Disguised Gardener's Girl*), at the Munich carnival. In his own words, it "turned out so well that I cannot possibly describe the storms of applause". Archbishop Colloredo came to Munich but did not see the opera and seemed indifferent to the

praises being heaped on his junior concert-master.

For the next two years Mozart stayed in Salzburg, composing busily but unhappy about being so far from Italy or the great courts of Europe and to be so little appreciated. When the Archbishop finally dismissed him from his service he sped off happily to Munich, with only his doting mother to keep him under control. Despite his reputation in Munich, no one would give him a job or commission an opera. It was the same in Augsburg, where he flirted with his cousin, Thekela, so Wolfgang and his mother moved on to Mannheim, where the local ruler's orchestra was reputed to be the finest in Europe. There was no

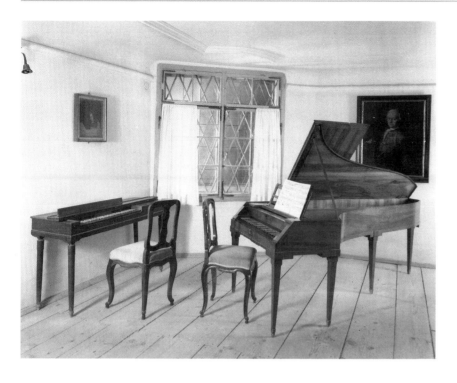

Mozart's piano and clavichord. Notice the portraits of Mozart (left, unfinished) **and of his father.**

job there either but the intense musical atmosphere led him into a whirlwind world of composing, playing, teaching, sightseeing and socializing. Living life on his own, free from the shadow of his sternly sensible father, Mozart fell suddenly and passionately in love. The girl, Aloysia Weber, was poor, pretty, 15 years old and had a beautiful singing voice. Mozart vowed to write arias that would make her famous. Leopold was horrified when he heard of their plans to tour Italy together and wrote a letter ordering Mozart and his mother to depart for Paris at once. They duly departed. Leopold's letter had been angry and to the point, warning his son of the danger of being "captured by some petticoat, bedded on straw and penned-in with an attic of starving children. Off with you to Paris and that soon! Find your place among great people. Aut Caesar aut nihil! (Either Caesar or nothing)."

In Paris Mozart pined for Aloysia and decided he hated everything French. Certainly the French at that time seemed to have little interest in him, though his symphony No. 31 did get a public performance and he also wrote a ballet, a concerto and seven sonatas for violin and piano.

The Mozarts lived poorly and Wolfgang's mother became ill. For three months her health grew steadily worse, until on 3 July 1778, she died in her son's arms. Grief stricken, Mozart turned for home. In Munich he found that Aloysia had become rich and famous without his help and no longer wanted to know him. Emotionally battered, the young adventurer returned to his birthplace.

A Question of Instruments

In the 18th Century a "clavier" meant a stringed keyboard instrument and could refer to any one of three main types:

Clavichord
A small piano-like instrument with a limited range of notes and a soft tone. When the player pressed a key, it made a brass blade strike a string. The harder the key was pressed, the higher the resulting note, but not the louder.

Harpsichord
This had a wider range of notes but, when the key was pressed, a string was plucked rather than struck. The result was that the player had less control over the tone and length of the note.

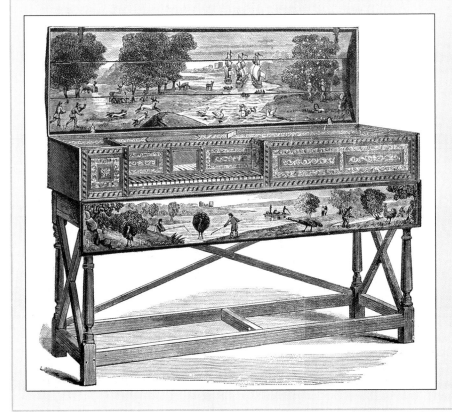

A mid-eighteenth century harpsichord. The earliest surviving example was made in Italy in 1521. Some had two "manuals" (keyboards).

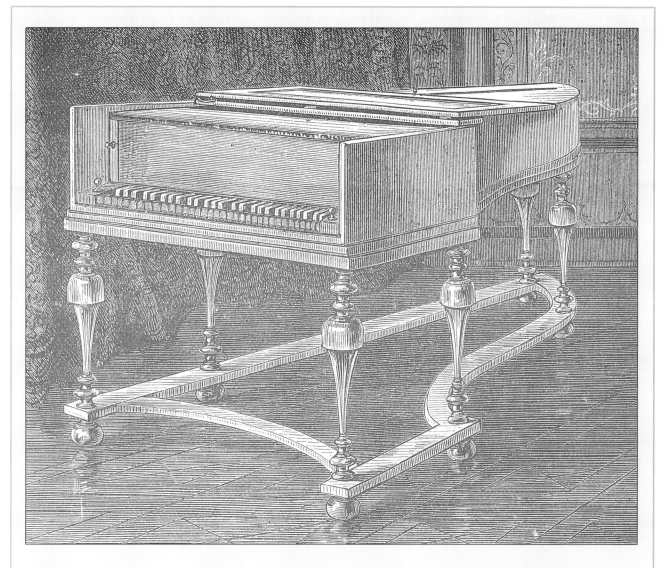

Pianoforte

This was invented in Florence by Bartolomeo Cristofori. The piano used a leather-covered hammer to strike the strings. This gave the player greater control over the tone, duration and loudness of a note and enabled notes to be played soft (piano) or loud (forte).

Mozart himself was especially interested in the technical aspects of keyboard instruments and was a great admirer of the pianos made by Andreas Stein of Augsburg. Although Mozart's father wanted him to concentrate on playing the violin, he preferred the piano.

An early piano, dated 1764, used by Mozart in the Town Hall at Potsdam, Prussia.

Struggling for Success

Mozart's disastrous expedition had plunged the family into debt and he was therefore obliged once again to accept a position in the service of the Archbishop. The court organist had recently died and Leopold managed to get the job for his wayward offspring. Father and son were united in their grief, their dislike of their employer and their devotion to music. But in other ways they were growing apart. Leopold despaired of his son's extravagant and untidy habits, symptoms of an inability to organize the details of his daily life. Wolfgang seldom argued back but moodily continued to do pretty much as he liked. Depressed and confined, he was once again immediately uplifted when he was asked to write yet another opera for the Munich carnival. In November 1780, the Archbishop gave him a brief leave of absence and he began work on *Idomeneo* which turned out to be another rousing success.

Mozart, exhilarated by renewed fame, overstayed his leave of absence by months and was abruptly summoned to join his master in Vienna. For three weeks he was sent to live with the servants and forbidden to accept invitations to play for other people. Then he was suddenly ordered back to Salzburg. He stayed put and after a series of heated arguments, he was literally kicked out of his job on 8 June 1781.

As far as Leopold was concerned this was bad enough. He had little love for the Archbishop but he recognized the value of a secure position, even if it was inglorious and underpaid. But worse was to follow. Wolfgang moved in with the Weber family, who were now living in Vienna and taking in lodgers. Madame Weber, a widow with three unmarried daughters, saw her opportunity. Wolfgang was treated like a lord and master. Leopold, fearing the worst, ordered him to change his lodgings. His son obeyed but it was already too late. He was now in love with Constanze Weber.

From Wolfgang's point of view, the world was a sunnier place altogether. He was free of the Archbishop. He was in love and was this time loved in return. He was paid well for teaching and gave concerts to packed audiences. His six new violin sonatas were an instant success, his brilliance as a performer was decisively proved by a celebrated "duel" with the pianist Muzio Clementi, organized at the invitation of the Emperor himself. Clementi conceded that he "had never before heard anyone play with such intelligence and grace".

Mozart also had another noteworthy achievement in 1781 — the composition of a revolutionary new

Constanze Mozart, — a charming scatter-brain, rather than the housekeeper Leopold wanted for his son.

Mozart's father in 1764. He gave up his own career for his gifted son.

opera set in a Turkish harem, *Die Entführung aus dem Serail (The Abduction from the Seraglio)*. It was revolutionary for two reasons. It was to be sung in German and not Italian and it actually required the main characters to act as well as sing. An opera would no longer consist of cardboard characters taking turns to sing to the audience. Henceforth, it would be a drama as well, in which words and music would represent the emotions of believable characters — even if they were often in fairly unbelievable situations.

In the meantime, the scheming Madame Weber hustled the giddy young musician into making a firm proposal of marriage to Constanze. Leopold was appalled and refused to give his consent. Wolfgang and Constanze waited until August 1782 and then went ahead with the wedding anyway. The harem opera had taken Vienna by storm. Goethe, Germany's greatest poet, said that it "put everything else in the shade". Surely its composer was now assured of a solid career? Was not the new emperor, Joseph II, a renowned music-lover?

If Mozart's father had hoped that a suitable wife might introduce some order into his son's life, he was to be disappointed. Constanze certainly loved her husband but she was just as incapable as he was of organizing either a budget or a household. For a while, the young couple could ignore such matters; teaching, performing and parties filled so much of their time. Then they had a son. Because he was so young, they left him in the care of a nurse while they visited Leopold in Salzburg. The visit was a fairly frosty affair, and when they returned to Vienna, they found that their baby had died while they were away. They were to have six children in all and four were to die in infancy. Constanze, for most of her married life was either having a baby or getting over the effects of the birth or death of one.

In the spring of 1784, Mozart fell seriously ill. He recovered slowly, ecouraged by the birth of a new son, Karl Thomas, who grew up to be a minor government official. In

Mozart at 33 — deeply in debt, his health already failing, he could still compose a great comic opera — and find relief in doing so.

January 1785, Leopold came to visit his son and grandson. On the evening of his arrival he went to see Wolfgang perform in concert. He was impressed by the music, the musicians and especially by the audience. Wolfgang introduced his father to Haydn who told him "your son is the greatest composer I know in person or by name". Mozart was to return the compliment by dedicating six string quartets to him — "most celebrated man and my dearest friend".

The young Mozarts' hectic lifestyle did not suit respectable, solid Leopold, as he made very clear in a letter to his daughter:

"We never get to bed before one o'clock at night, never rise before nine ... There are concerts every day, lessons all the time, composing and so on ... It is impossible to describe the fuss and the noise."

In May 1785, Leopold went home to Salzburg. Wolfgang was never to see either his father or his birthplace again.

Freemasonry

The Freemasons are a society whose members are dedicated to helping each other and supporting charity. Members are required to believe in a Supreme Being, the immortality of the soul and obedience to the law. Freemasonry is not a religion as such but members are required to go through various rituals to become members of a lodge. The Roman Catholic church disapproves of Freemasonry but did not do so in Vienna in the 1780s. So Mozart, who joined a lodge in 1784, could be both a good Catholic and a Freemason.

In Germany, the great poets Goethe and Herder were both Freemasons. In Vienna itself, the Emperor Joseph was a member and so were Gluck and Haydn. Mozart even persuaded his father to join. Leopold was probably impressed by the distinguished company he would be keeping.

Freemasonry affected Mozart's life in two ways, apart from the friends it brought him. As he fell deeper into debt, he came to rely heavily on loans from a fellow Mason, Michael Puchberg, a banker. It is also said that his operas contain secret references to Masonic beliefs and symbols.

Johann Wolfgang von Goethe (1749-1832) Germany's great man of letters. A lover of Italy like Mozart, he was also a poet whose lyrics were often set to music.

Struggling for Survival

Mozart was usually dutiful in writing to his father regularly, but Leopold heard not a word from him throughout the spring and summer of 1785. The young composer was simply obsessed with his latest project, a comic opera called *The Marriage of Figaro*. Based on a hugely successful play by the French writer, Beaumarchais, it was to be rewritten for the opera stage by Lorenzo da Ponte, an Italian who had just been appointed as Joseph II's official theatre poet, and was to be Mozart's most successful collaborator.

Mozart and Da Ponte worked well together, matching witty words with bright music. The première on 1 May 1786, was Mozart's greatest triumph yet, as the Irish singer, Michael Kelly (Mozart's billiards' opponent) enthusiastically recorded: "I thought the audience would never be done applauding and calling for Mozart; almost every piece was encored, which prolonged it nearly to the length of three operas ... "

If *The Marriage of Figaro* was a triumph in Vienna, in Prague it was a miracle. Mozart hurried to the city and found that:

"Here they talk nothing but Figaro; scrape, blow, sing and whistle nothing but Figaro; no opera draws but Figaro, always Figaro". Unfortunately, this great success brought him not a single penny.

After a wonderful month in Prague, Mozart returned to Vienna with a commission to write yet another opera, the story of the

The title page of an early German edition of *The Marriage of Figaro*.

legendary womaniser, Don Juan — *Don Giovanni*. Mozart and da Ponte worked at top speed until the strain, added to constant worries about money and Constanze's health, forced the composer to set the work aside. Worse still, when he learned that his father had fallen seriously ill, he was too ill himself to go and see him. By the time Wolfgang had recovered, Leopold had died and been buried.

Don Giovanni was finished in a great rush, with Mozart putting the last touches to the overture on the morning of the first performance. The première, in Prague on October 29, was another wild success. Leopold would, no doubt, have been proud had he lived to see it. But he would have been even prouder of the fact that, when Gluck died in

November 1787, it was Wolfgang Amadeus Mozart who was appointed to succeed him as "Imperial and Royal Court Composer". Mozart's appointment bought him honour but very little wealth as the Emperor paid him less than half what he had paid Gluck. He also had the endless chore of writing trivial pieces for dances and court entertainment. The composer made his feelings about such tasks quite clear by sending back a receipt for his salary with a note "Too much for what I do — Too little for what I could do". It has been well said that Mozart was a courtly composer, not because he served kings and princes but because his music had the polish and elegance of a truly refined taste.

(Left) **Title page of the vocal score of *Don Giovanni*. (Breitkopf and Härtel later published a complete edition of Mozart's works.)** (Right) **Modern poster for *Idomeneo*.**

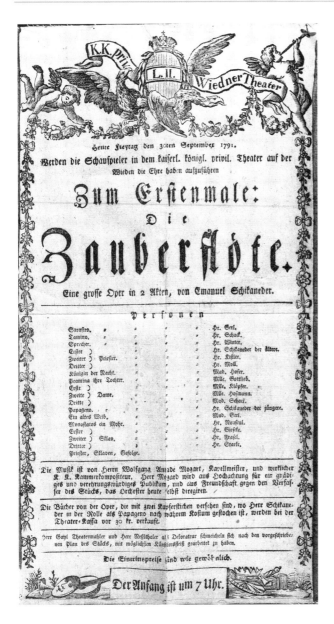

A poster for the première of *The Magic Flute*. Note that Schikaneder ranks above Mozart in the billing.

three great symphonies, Nos. 39-41, which were to be his last. But it was teaching and performing, rather than composing, that kept the family finances afloat. And since the house in the country was too far for pupils to come, it was back to a flat in the city — the eleventh time the Mozarts had moved house since their marriage.

The return to Vienna did not, however, revive Mozart's fortunes. His concerts no longer attracted large audiences. Another major source of income was drying up. He had to borrow from friends to pay his household bills. Then in April 1789, his friend and former pupil, Prince Karl Lichnowsky, organized a concert tour for him. In Leipzig he had the chance to play Johann Sebastian Bach's very own church organ, and in Berlin he was commissioned to compose six string quartets and six piano sonatas. But when he returned to Vienna a month later, he had little more money than when he started.

No sooner had he returned than Constanze fell seriously ill and Mozart had to borrow yet again to pay for medicines and doctors. By July 1789 he was writing in desperation to his friend Michael Puchberg "I would not wish my worst enemy to be in my present position. And if you, beloved friend and brother, forsake me, we are altogether lost, both my unfortunate and blameless self and my poor sick wife and child".

He found distraction from his

In June 1788, the Mozarts moved out of the city to save money on rent. Ten days after the move, their baby daughter Theresa died. Despite his sadness and his never ending worries about money, Mozart, in the course of just over a month, composed no fewer than

A poster for a modern production of *The Magic Flute*. (The eye at the top is a Masonic symbol.)

troubles by working on yet another opera — *Cosi fan Tutte* (*They all Behave Thus*).

In February 1790, the Emperor, Joseph II, died, and with him died Mozart's position as court composer. The Emperor's death also meant the closure of all theatres for a period of mourning. This ended the new opera's run after only nine performances. Mozart fretted throughout the rest of the year, wondering whether the new emperor would reappoint him. The worry made him ill, with constant headaches and sleepless nights. In

September he set out for Frankfurt where Leopold II was to have his coronation. Mozart had no official invitation and had to pawn his family silver to pay for the journey, as well as borrow yet more money to make up the rest of what he needed.

In Frankfurt, he gave a concert which gained him much praise but very little cash. He went on to Mannheim, but it was the same there. Back in Vienna he set about completing another opera *The Magic Flute*. The libretto was written in German by an actor friend of Mozart's, Emanuel Schikaneder. It was he who suggested the idea in the first place and who was to play one of the leading parts in the first performance.

In July 1791, Constanze gave birth to another son, whom they called Franz Xavier Wolfgang (calling himself Wolfgang Jr., he grew up to become a composer). At about the same time a mysterious stranger in grey called on Mozart with an anonymous letter, asking him to compose a requiem mass. The author of the letter was actually a nobleman, Count Walsegg, who wanted to pass the composition off as his own, written to mourn the death of his wife. Mozart, who felt that he was now losing his own struggle for survival, began to look on the strange project as an invitation from destiny. In September, he wrote to da Ponte:

"I am on the point of expiring. My end has come before I was able to profit by my talent. And yet life has been so beautiful ... But no one can change his fate ... Before me lies my swan song. I must not leave it incomplete".

At the same time, he was also working frantically to finish *The Magic Flute*, completing the score the day before the première. Its instant success lifted his spirits and he began to talk about going back to England the following year to take up generous invitations to compose and perform. But his illness had taken too firm a grip for him to shake it off. He had fainting fits and was convinced that he was being poisoned. In fact he was suffering from a renewed bout of rheumatic fever, which had strained his heart when he was young. On 20 November 1791, he took to his bed. His doctor's treatment of bloodletting weakened his condition still further. On 4 December he gave detailed instructions on how his requiem should be finished to one of his pupils, Süssmayr. He died early the next morning, probably of kidney failure, aged 35.

Mozart was buried in a pauper's grave at public expense. Neither family nor friends were present at his burial. No cross marked his resting place. His music must remain his epitaph.

Mozart's memorial in Vienna. A broken column was a traditional symbol for a young life cut short.

Find Out More ...

Important Books

Mozart by Wolfgang Hildesheimer (Dent, 1983)

Mozart by Ian McLean (Hamlyn, 1990)

Letters of Wolfgang Amadeus Mozart ed. by Hans Mersmann (Dover, 1972)

Mozart: The Golden Years by H.C. Robbins Landon (Thames & Hudson, 1989)

Mozart: A Bicentennial Tribute by Wendy Thompson (Apple Tree Press, 1990)

Composer's World: Mozart by Wendy Thompson (Faber & Faber, 1990)

Mozart: His Life and Times by Peggy Woodford (Omnibus, 1984)

Important Addresses

University of Edinburgh
Collection of Historic Musical
  Instruments
Reid Concert Hall
Bristo Square
Edinburgh EH8 9AG

Royal College of Music
Museum of Instruments
Prince Consort Road
London SW7 2BS

Important Dates

1756 Born in Salzburg
1762 Visits Munich and Vienna
1763 Begins European tour
1764 Lives in London
1768 Visits Vienna
1769 First opera *La Finta Semplice* performed in public
1770 Tours Italy
1771 *Ascanio in Alba*
1772 Count von Colloredo becomes Archbishop of Salzburg; *Lucio Silla*
1774 Visits Vienna
1775 *La Finta Giardiniera*
1776 Visits Salzburg
1777 Leaves service of the Archbishop for the first time; falls in love with Aloysia Weber
1778 Death of his mother in Paris
1779 Returns to the service of the Archbishop

1780 Composes *Idomeneo*
1781 Dismissed by Archbishop Colloredo
1782 Marries Constanze Weber
1783 Visit to Leopold in Salzburg
1784 Birth of his son, Karl; becomes a Freemason
1785 Last visit from Leopold
1786 *The Marriage of Figaro*
1787 *Don Giovanni*; appointed Court Composer; death of Leopold Mozart
1788 Death of daughter Theresa; composes symphonies 39-41
1789 Concert tour with Prince Lichnowsky
1790 *Cosi Fan Tutte*; attends coronation of Leopold II
1791 Birth of son, Franz Xavier; *The Magic Flute*; Dies.

Glossary

Aria   Italian word for a song, usually used to describe an extended air by a single voice in an opera. In Mozart's time, this usually involved a first movement, a contrasting second part and a repeat of the first part, usually with variations to show off the singer's skill.

Carnival   A festival time with many parties and special occasions, usually just before Lent, a period of abstinence in the Christian calendar.

Concerto   A piece of music which enables a solo instrument to show off its range and skill, against the contrasting accompaniment of an orchestra.

Improvise   To play without written music, that is, make up the music as one goes along.

Libretto   The text or book of the spoken words of an opera, oratorio or ballet.

Modulation   A technical term when the music being played changes from one key to another using chords which link the two keys.

Quartet   Music written to be played by a group of four performers. A string quartet consists of two violins, a viola and a cello.

Sonata   A musical composition written for a solo instrument.

Symphony   A complex piece of music written for a whole orchestra. In Mozart's time, it consisted of four parts (movements).

Index

Picture Acknowledgements

The publishers would like to thank the following for their kind permission to reproduce their photographs in this book: Austrian Tourist Board 7 (bottom), 10 (bottom), 29; Hunterian Art Gallery/University of Glasgow 19; Internationale Stiftung Mozarteum Salzburg 4,6,8,10 (top), 13,15,26; Mary Evans Picture Library cover, 7 (top), 11,16,17,22,31; Peter Bull Art Studio maps 9,12; Royal College of Music frontispiece, 5,14,20,21,23,24; courtesy of the Royal Opera House, London/Jane Ray 27; courtesy of the Royal Opera House, London/Irene von Treskow 25.